The Hedgosaurus
Toby Glover©2023

Happy World Book Day!
Toby :)

Rony has a secret
Which he's dying to share
But he could never tell anyone
He just wouldn't dare

Outside in his garden
Right down at the end
That's where he lives
His secret friend Steg

He's only a baby one
But Rony is sure
His secret new friend
Is a young dinosaur

Steg is still very small
Much smaller than us
But when he grows up
He'll be as big as a bus

Steg likes to snuffle
With his cute tiny jaws
But when he grows up
He'll let out a huge roar

Steg eats moss and fern
And frogs snails and berries
But loves insects the most
They fill up his belly

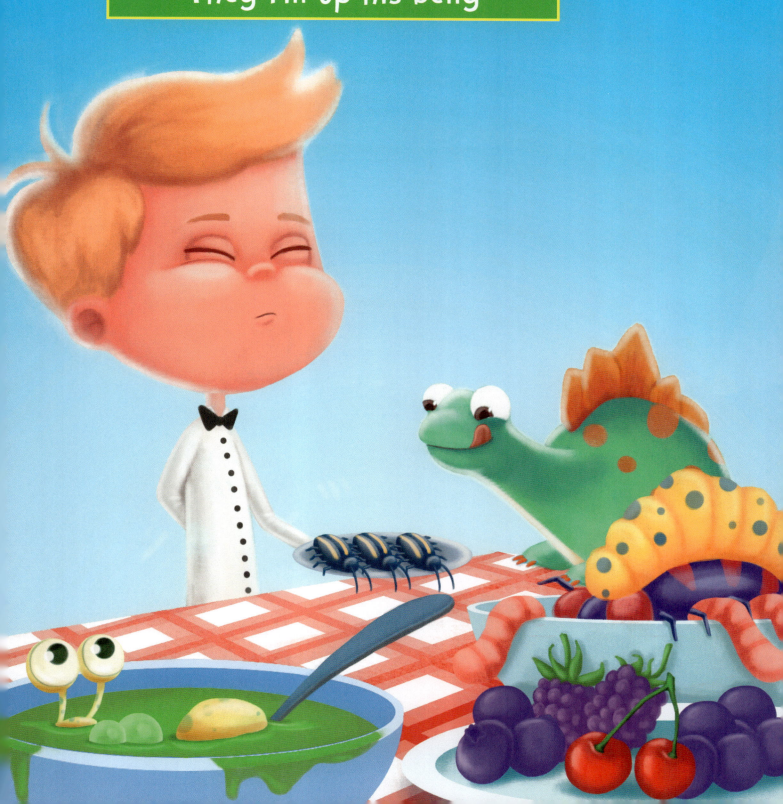

He also loves earthworms
So Rony stamps on the ground
They think it's a rainstorm
Then Steg munches them down

Rony loves Steg
And Steg loves him back
If they ever split up
Rony's heart would crack

"So that's who you play with?
When it's time for your bed
Then please introduce us,"
His Mum and Dad said

BUT STEG HAD GONE!!!

Rony spent all that winter
Searching for Steg
But it was cold in the garden
So Mum would send him to bed

Rony missed Steg so much
He was sad for so long
He just did not know
Where his best friend had gone

Then his teacher was ill
So the class had another
He was nice he was kind
He was called Mr Glover

He saw Rony was sad
So he asked him why?
So Rony talked about Steg
Then he started to cry

So Rony felt a bit better
He now understood
That his friend went away
But had not gone for good

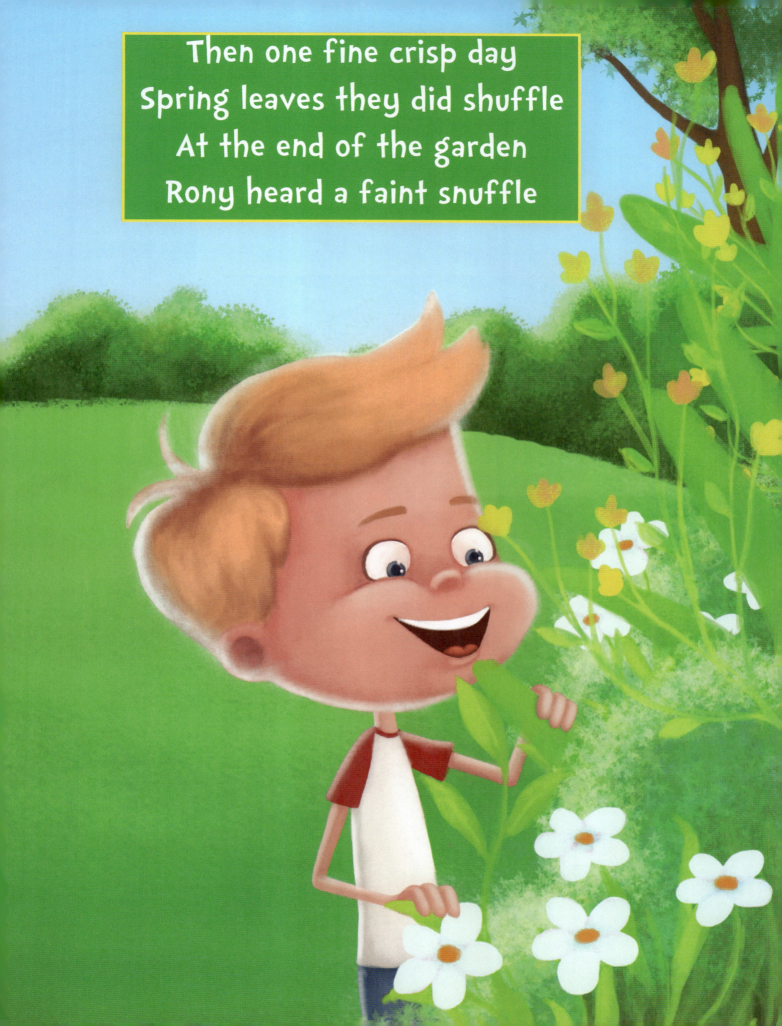

Out popped a black snout
Then two shiny eyes
His best friend was back
He had doubled in size

Rony felt delighted
To see his old friend
Two friends reunited
'Til the very end

And now Rony's a grown-up
He's older, he's wise
Steg's grown up too
He's not quite the same size

Rony's new garden is massive
It's huge, it's enormous
The perfect new home
For his pet Stegosaurus!

fin

For more of Toby's stories, just scan the code!

Printed in Great Britain
by Amazon